Hello

Kelly Doudna

ABDO Publishing Company

Published by SandCastle™, an imprint of ABDO Publishing Company, 4940 Viking Drive, Edina, Minnesota 55435.

Printed in the United States.

Cover and interior photo credits: Eyewire Images, Digital Stock, PhotoDisc, Stock Market

Library of Congress Cataloging-in-Publication Data

Doudna, Kelly, 1963-
    Hello / Kelly Doudna.
        p. cm. -- (Good manners)
    Includes index.
    ISBN 1-57765-575-3
        1. Courtesy--Juvenile literature. 2. Children--Conduct of life. 3. Etiquette. [1.
Etiquette.] I. Title.

BJ1533.C9 .D684 2001
395.1'22--dc21
                                                                        2001022005

The SandCastle concept, content, and reading method have been reviewed and approved by a national advisory board including literacy specialists, librarians, elementary school teachers, early childhood education professionals, and parents.

Let Us Know

After reading the book, SandCastle would like you to tell us your stories about reading. What is your favorite page? Was there something hard that you needed help with? Share the ups and downs of learning to read. We want to hear from you! To get posted on the ABDO Publishing Company Web site, send us email at:

sandcastle@abdopub.com

About SandCastle™
Nonfiction books for the beginning reader

- Basic concepts of phonics are incorporated with integrated language methods of reading instruction. Most words are short, and phrases, letter sounds, and word sounds are repeated.

- Readability is determined by the number of words in each sentence, the number of characters in each word, and word lists based on curriculum frameworks.

- Full-color photography reinforces word meanings and concepts.

- "Words I Can Read" list at the end of each book teaches basic elements of grammar, helps the reader recognize the words in the text, and builds vocabulary.

- Reading levels are indicated by the number of flags on the castle.

Look for more SandCastle books
in these three reading levels:

Level 1 (one flag)	Level 2 (two flags)	Level 3 (three flags)

Grades Pre-K to K 5 or fewer words per page	**Grades K to 1** 5 to 10 words per page	**Grades 1 to 2** 10 to 15 words per page

We say "hello" when
we want to greet another
person or get their attention.

We say "hello" to show that we have good manners.

Julio gives his grandfather
a kiss.

He says, "**Hello**, Grandpa.
I am happy to see you."

Matt whispers into a pretend phone.

He asks, "**Hello**? Can anybody hear me?"

Tim turns around.

He heard his friend shout, "Hello, Tim. Wait for me!"

Bonita sneaks up behind her dad.

She says, "**Hello**! Guess who!"

Pete plays with his friends.

He says, "**Hello**, Holly.
Hello, Helen."

The Chens answer the door.

The delivery person says,
"**Hello**. Here is your pizza."

Will wants to talk to his friend on the phone.

What should he say?

Words I Can Read

Nouns
A noun is a person, place, or thing

attention (uh-TEN-shuhn) p. 5
dad (DAD) p. 15
door (DOR) p. 19
friend (FREND) pp. 13, 21
grandfather (GRAND-fah-thur) p. 9
kiss (KISS) p. 9
person (PUR-suhn) pp. 5, 19
phone (FOHN) pp. 11, 21
pizza (PEET-suh) p. 19

Proper Nouns
A proper noun is the name of a person, place, or thing

Bonita (boh-NEE-tuh) p. 15
Chens (CHENZ) p. 19
Grandpa (GRAND-pah) p. 9
Helen (HEL-in) p. 17
Holly (HOL-ee) p. 17
Julio (HOO-lee-oh) p. 9
Matt (MAT) p. 11
Pete (PEET) p. 17
Tim (TIM) p. 13
Will (WIL) p. 21

Plural Nouns
A plural noun is more than one person, place, or thing

friends (FRENDZ) p. 17
manners (MAN-urz) p. 7

Pronouns
A pronoun is a word that replaces a noun

anybody (EN-ee-bod-ee) p. 11
he (HEE) pp. 9, 11, 13, 17, 21
I (EYE) p. 9
me (MEE) pp. 11, 13
she (SHEE) p. 15
we (WEE) pp. 5, 7
what (WUHT) p. 21
who (HOO) p. 15
you (YOO) p. 9

Verbs

A verb is an action or being word

am (AM) p. 9	**hear** (HIHR) p. 11	**show** (SHOH) p. 7
answer (AN-sur) p. 19	**heard** (HURD) p. 13	**sneaks** (SNEEKSS) p. 15
asks (ASKSS) p. 11	**is** (IZ) p. 19	**talk** (TAWK) p. 21
can (KAN) p. 11	**plays** (PLAYZ) p. 17	**turns** (TURNZ) p. 13
get (GET) p. 5	**say** (say) pp. 5, 7 , 21	**wait** (WATE) p. 13
gives (GIVZ) p. 9	**says** (SEZ) pp. 9, 15, 17, 19	**want** (WONT) p. 5
greet (GREET) p. 5	**see** (SEE) p. 9	**wants** (WONTSS) p. 21
guess (GESS) p. 15	**should** (SHUD) p. 21	**whispers** (WISS-purz) p. 11
have (HAV) p. 7	**shout** (SHOUT) p. 13	

Adjectives

An adjective describes something

another (uh-NUTH-UR) p. 5	**good** (GUD) p. 7	**pretend** (pri-TEND) p. 11
delivery (di-LIV-ur-ee) p. 19	**happy** (HAP-ee) p. 9	**their** (THAIR) p. 5
	her (HUR) p. 15	**your** (YOR) p. 19
	his (HIZ) pp. 9, 13, 17, 21	

Adverbs

An adverb tells how, when, or where something happens

around (uh-ROUND) p. 13	**behind** (be-HINDE) p. 15	**out** (OUT) p. 13
	here (HIHR) p. 19	**up** (UHP) p. 15

23

Glossary

delivery person – someone who takes something to someone.

manners – polite behavior.

pretend – make believe.

sneaks – moves quietly and secretly.

whispers – talks very quietly or softly.